Contents

What is health?   6

Why do we need to eat?   8

When should we eat?   10

How much water should we drink?   12

Why must we clean our teeth?   14

Why must we wash with soap?   16

Why do our nails need cutting?   18

Why must we wash and brush our hair?   20

Why must we protect our skin from the sun?   22

Why is exercise good for us?   24

How can I get better if I am ill?   26

Glossary   28

Index   29

Animal index and quiz   30

What is health?

A healthy person feels well and is full of energy.

Our bodies need care to stay healthy. We must keep clean, eat the right food, take exercise and rest. When we are not healthy, we can easily become ill.

When did you last have a cold or flu? How did you get better? How long did it take before you were well again?

6

Humans and Other Animals
Keeping Healthy

David and Penny Glover

W
FRANKLIN WATTS
LONDON•SYDNEY

First published in 2004 by
Franklin Watts
96 Leonard Street
London
EC2A 4XD

Franklin Watts Australia
45-51 Huntley Street
Alexandria
NSW 2015

Series Editor: Sally Luck
Art Director: Jonathan Hair
Design: Matthew Lilly

ISBN 0 7496 5546 1

All photographs taken by Ray Moller unless
otherwise credited.

John Cancalosi/Still Pictures: 9b, 23b.
Mark Carwardine/Still Pictures: 9t.
T & P Gardner/FLPA: 25t.
Michael Gore/Ecoscene: 21t.
Eric & David Hosking/FLPA: 7b, 11t.
Klein Hubert/Still Pictures: 11b.
M.&C.Denis-Huot/Still Pictures: 15b, 25b.
E A Janes/RSPCA Photolibrary: 13t.
Gerard Lacz/FLPA: front cover r, 7t, 19b.
Mike Lane/NHPA: 13b.
Andy Rouse/NHPA: 19t.
Silvestris/FLPA: 15t.
Jurgen & Christine Sohns/FLPA: 17t.
John Watkins/FLPA: 23t.
Bill Wood/NHPA: 17b.
Norbert Wu/Still Pictures: 21b.

Every attempt has been made to clear
copyright. Should there be any inadvertent
omission, please apply to the publisher for
rectification

A CIP catalogue record for this book is
available from the British Library.

Printed in Hong Kong / China

A healthy horse is well fed. Its eyes are bright, its coat shines and it is full of energy. It loves to gallop in the field.

When there is drought in hot countries, animals cannot find enough food or water. They are not healthy. They move slowly, their ribs stick out and their coats are dull.

Why do we need to eat?

Food is fuel.
It gives our bodies
energy and the things
we need to grow
and stay healthy.

It is important to eat a mix
of foods, including fruit
and vegetables. They
contain lots of vitamins
and minerals which help
our bodies to work well.

What is your favourite fruit? What is your
favourite vegetable? How many fruits and
vegetables do you eat each day? You should
try to eat at least five different kinds.

Like humans, a brown bear is an omnivore. Omnivores eat a mix of foods. As well as roots and fruit, a bear likes honey from bees' nests, and fish from the river.

Spiders are carnivores. Carnivores only eat other animals. This giant tarantula from South America is as big as a dinner plate. It eats small birds, mice and frogs!

When should we eat?

We should eat at meal times –
breakfast in the morning,
lunch at mid-day,
and an evening meal.

Breakfast gives us energy to start the day.
Eating just snacks, such as crisps, instead of
proper meals is not healthy. Snacks do not
give us all the vitamins and minerals we need.

What do you call the meals you eat each day? When do you eat them? Write out your menu for the day. Do you think it is healthy?

Animals do not eat at meal times like we do. A caterpillar eats leaves all day long - non-stop! It does this to get the energy it needs to make its body grow.

In the autumn, a dormouse eats as much as it can. This food turns into fat. The extra fat helps the dormouse survive in winter, when there's not much food around.

11

How much water should we drink?

We should drink
about 2 litres
of water a day.

Our bodies lose water when
we sweat or go to the toilet.
There is water in the air we
breathe out, too. If we do not
replace this water, we become
dehydrated and our bodies
do not work properly.

Some foods, like fruit and soup,
contain water. Squeeze the
juice from an orange. How
much juice does it contain? Use
a measuring jug to find out.

If you keep a pet, such as a budgie, you must make sure it always has clean water to drink. Without water most animals will die in just a few days.

Camels live in hot, dry deserts. They can go for over two weeks without water! They carry fat in their humps. This food supply helps them survive when there is nothing to eat or drink.

13

Why must we clean our teeth?

If we do not clean our teeth, they rot, ache and give us smelly breath!

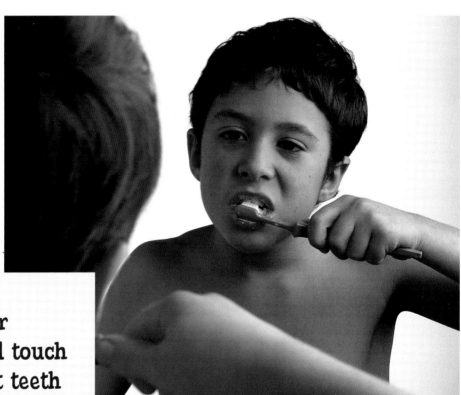

Wash your hands and touch your front teeth with a finger. Do they feel smooth and clean, or dirty? Brush your teeth and feel them again. How do they feel now?

When we eat, tiny scraps of food get left on our teeth. Germs feed on these scraps and make plaque that rots our teeth. We should clean our teeth each morning and night to brush food scraps away.

A shark does not need to clean its rows of fierce teeth. When its front teeth wear down or break, new teeth move forwards from the rows behind to fill the gaps.

A Nile crocodile has a strange way of cleaning its teeth. It lets the tooth-picker bird take food scraps from between its teeth. The crocodile does not mind - this stops it getting toothache!

Why must we wash with soap?

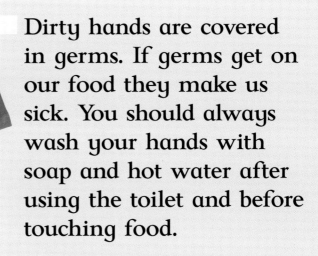

Soap and hot water wash harmful germs from your skin.

Dirty hands are covered in germs. If germs get on our food they make us sick. You should always wash your hands with soap and hot water after using the toilet and before touching food.

Make your hands dirty with wet newspaper. Wash them with cold water. Wash them with hot water and soap. Which works best?

A sparrow does not wash with soap. Instead, it takes a dust bath in dry mud! The dust helps to clean parasites (tiny creatures that infect the skin) from the sparrow's feathers.

Cleaner fish help keep bigger fish free from parasites. The cleaner fish eats the parasites. The big fish thanks the cleaner fish by not eating it!

Why do our nails need cutting?

Our nails never stop growing. If we don't cut them, they get dirty and carry germs.

Our nails protect the tips of our fingers and toes. They are useful tools too. Nails help us scratch an itch or pull a splinter from our skin.

Ask an adult to mark one of your fingernails with a thin line of nail varnish. Watch how the line moves as your nail grows. How far does it move in a week?

Badgers use their strong front claws to dig for food. They also use them to dig the tunnels in which they live. A badger's claws get worn down by digging, so they do not need to be cut.

A cat uses its claws to catch its prey. Cats keep their claws sharp by scratching rough surfaces like wood. When it is not hunting, a cat can pull its claws back inside its foot to stop them becoming blunt.

19

Why must we wash and brush our hair?

Keeping our hair clean is important. It helps to keep us free of parasites such as head lice. It makes us look nice too!

Head lice are tiny insects that live in human hair. They lay eggs called nits. Lots of children catch head lice at school. But you can easily get rid of them with special shampoo and a fine comb.

Apes often have parasites such as lice and fleas in their fur. This makes their skin itchy. Apes pick out the parasites from each other's fur. This is called grooming.

The tree sloth doesn't mind having dirty fur. It lets green algae (a kind of plant) grow in its fur. This makes the sloth look green, which helps it to hide in the trees!

Make a list of animals with fur and animals without fur. How do animals with fur look after their coats?

21

Why must we protect our skin from the sun?

The sun can burn our skin. Sunburn is very painful and it can make us ill, too.

When we go out in the sun we should wear a hat to shade our heads. We should put sun cream on bare skin.

Strong sun creams have high factor numbers. Children should use Factor 30 sun cream. Can you find out what Factor 30 means?

A white pig can easily get sunburnt. Rolling in wet mud cools the pig down and helps to protect its skin. The layer of dried mud on its back blocks the bright sunlight!

Lizards do not need to protect their tough scaly skin. They love to bask in the hot sun. It warms up their cold bodies.

Why is exercise good for us?

Exercise makes our hearts and muscles strong.

Exercise makes your heart beat faster. When you finish exercising your heart slows down again. Sports and games are good exercise. So are walking and cycling.

Put your hand flat on your chest. Can you feel your heart beating? Now jog for two minutes. How does your heart beat change? Stay still for two minutes and feel it again. How does it feel now?

As young eaglets grow in their nest, they practise flapping their wings. This exercise helps to make their wing muscles strong enough for flying.

An adult cheetah can run at speeds of 110 kilometres per hour. It is the fastest runner in the world! A young cheetah exercises hard so that it, too, can grow as strong and fast as its parents.

How can I get better if I am ill?

You must always tell an adult when you feel ill. They will help you get better.

Everyone gets ill from time to time. We may have a stomach ache or catch a cold. Our body can often fight an illness by itself. After resting we may start to feel better.

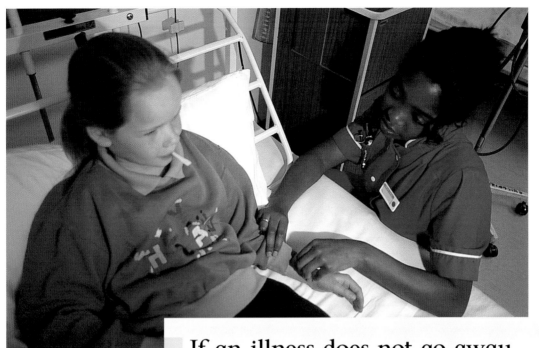

If an illness does not go away, you must visit the doctor. A doctor will decide what is wrong and may give you some medicine. Sometimes you have to visit the hospital for tests.

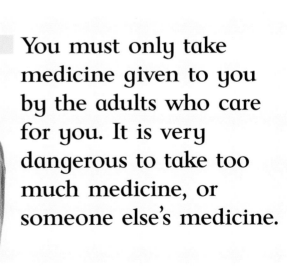

You must only take medicine given to you by the adults who care for you. It is very dangerous to take too much medicine, or someone else's medicine.

Glossary

carnivore
An animal that only eats other animals.

dehydrated
When the body has not got enough water in it, it is dehydrated. A dehydrated body does not work properly.

drought
A long period of time when there is no rain.

germ
A tiny living thing that causes disease.

plaque
Plaque rots our teeth. We get plaque on our teeth if we don't clean them properly.

mineral
Your body needs minerals to help it grow and stay healthy. Minerals are found in some foods.

omnivore
An animal that eats a mixture of plant and animal foods.

parasite
A tiny creature that lives on or in the body of another living thing, causing it harm.

vitamins
Your body needs vitamins to keep it healthy. Vitamins are found in some foods, such as fruit and vegetables.

28

Index

carnivore 9
claws 19

dehydrated 12
drought 7

energy 6, 7, 8, 10, 11
exercise 6, 24, 25

germs 14, 16, 18

ill 6, 22, 26, 27

meals 10, 11
medicine 27
minerals 8, 10

nails 18

omnivore 9

parasites 17, 20, 21
pet 13

soap 16, 17
sun 22, 23

teeth 14, 15

vitamins 8, 10

water 7, 12, 13, 16

Animal index and quiz

antelope 7
ape 21

badger 19
bear 9
budgie 13

camel 13
cat 19
caterpillar 11

cheetah 25
crocodile 15

dormouse 11

eaglet 25

fish 17

horse 7

lizard 23

pig 23

shark 15
sparrow 17

tarantula 9
tree sloth 21

Use your animal index to find the answers to this animal quiz!

How does a crocodile clean its teeth?

How does a sparrow keep clean?

How does a pig protect its skin from the sun?

What would you find in a tree sloth's hair?

What do tarantulas in South America eat?

How long can a camel go without water?